Apricity

Pavaki Nanda

For my Nana, who inspired me to write.

~P.N.D, you'll live in our hearts forever

Contents

This book is a labor of love, something I've been compiling over the past few years. It's an expression of my grief, sorrow, healing, self-discovery, and how I've processed the world around me. The pieces within are born from curiosity, adventure, and deep, thought-provoking conversations—my personal way of navigating complex emotions and, honestly, the whirlwind of teenage years.

Throughout this past year, I've experienced many phases—joy, loss, failure—and each poem reflects a part of that journey. Through my writing, I hope some of you find comfort in knowing you're not alone in feeling what you feel.

The word "Apricity" is one I hold close to my heart, though it's a word that has been largely forgotten by dictionaries. Its meaning, however, is powerful and beautiful. Apricity is the warmth of sunlight on a cold winter day, much like how writing became my ray of light during moments of darkness. Every day is apricity—a new beginning, a fresh chapter, the first day of the rest of your life.

So, contemplate, curate and celebrate!

Cheers!

– **Pavaki Nanda**

Apricity. A ray of sunshine of warm sunshine on a cold winter's day. A word that completely shattered my heart yet put back together as well. It's a coin with two opposite sides. My relationship with the word cannot be understood or explained. It is both the wound and the aid. It is midnight yet as bright as the sun. It is love and it is hope.

I came upon the word Apricity by some fateful chance. It is a word forgone by dictionaries, forgotten by people and its beauty and clarity has been lost to a yellowing page in history. It is so powerful yet rife with imperfection- a description of an illusionary hope that is, winter sunshine.

To me, this word is hope. It is a belief that no matter how thickly laid the snow may be, no matter how dense the fog, no matter how bleak the winter hail, no matter how dark the night- hope prevails each time. It's light bursts through the darkest of nights, saves from the deepest trenches of sorrow, it rises promptly to the occasion of day, airing out all the fog and hail. It surpasses even rain. It is hope that shatters a person's soul, the evillest entity to exist and yet hope is what wins and losses wars and hope that will make Apricity shine once again.

Apricity is a symbol of love, guiding one through grief. Grief that is overwhelming and all-consuming, grief like an overflowing well.

"You are Apricity, a face of evil in eternity,

you're both love and hope, you are everything in between"

– Pavaki Nanda

Musings

Confessions of a Writer

Every day I write a poem or two,
Twining together threads of perception,
Speeding along on the train of thought,
Hoping each sprinting feeling is caught.

I find inspiration at the oddest of times,
Waking up in a spell in the middle of the night,
My whizzing pen in class is just a guise,
For the words I weave in the light of sunrise.

A word or a sound could suddenly strike,
A sentence or a song heard riding a bike,
Each blade of grass finds its way onto the page,
As I dream of writing each hour of each day.

05.08.2024

Music

Thumping beats and electric sounds,
Invade the heart to its deepest depths,
Some songs slow down to show me dreams,
Some beats make me lose my breath.

Music fills my eardrums with a buzz,
A cacophony of tunes- melodies and such,
Music makes me light up like a match,
A fire that doesn't need alcohol's buzz.

Music makes me glimpse glittering dreams,
It makes me wanna feel alive,
It ignites the passion to step out- shout aloud,
It plays the reel of a wonderful life.

Euphoria rushes in at the sound of dancing shoes,
Flushed faces in a blur surround me,
Flickering lights reflect off of shimmying bodies,
Intoxicated emotions, finally set free.

My ears turn red, my hearts thumps along,
To the drums of a carnival band,
And my wishes come to life in front of my eyes,
As I repeat- black coat, black shoes, black hat Cadillac.

06.10.2024

Assuming the Worst

The world's taught me to assume the worst,
Leaping to endless conclusions,
Flipping a switch in my brain,
Training me to live in illusion.

I can no longer fathom what's true what's not,
Sincerity seems like a farce,
Genuine sorrow seems like an act,
Something I dissect into parts.

No longer do I administer the joy I receive,
It all seems like a jealous feat,
The actions of others no longer seem bright,
Victory is achieved only to compete.

24.08.24

Golgappa is an Emotion

Golgappa is an emotion

Crispy, golden-brown perfection,
Round and fried with a tangy temptation,
With stuffing so soft it's worth a mention,
Each bite is an experience, each chew a sensation.

Pani-puri, golgappe, phuchke -what to choose?
With an array of mouthwatering spices and hues.
Each night and day I'm reminded of you,
Each rainy day is incomplete without you.

Golgappa is not a just a savoury treat,
It's a reward, a celebration- only worth eating on the street.
It's a staple to beat away the heat,
Golgappa is an emotion, spicy and sweet.

16.06.2024

Facades

What it is really that we perceive of humanity?

We make up stories and fantasies of what they're like.

Without truly knowing a person, all we know of them is what we've
created,

We're nothing but creations ourselves.

Human nature as we call it invents and reinvents
itself to cater to the world,

But the world is really what we see it or shall I say imagine it to be.

Without truly knowing a person all we have is our story of them,

We create a rendition of the person they really are.

Is it fallacy, insanity, profanity?

I asked myself the same.

Truly there is nothing to know about a being with
their masks of camouflage,

But when they take it off are we ever truly ready to face the reality?

When the farce falls away, the masks slip and the truth appears,

Can we become accustomed to the naked reality we are confronted by?

That's the real question.

In the end what are we but figments of imagination?

Characters and ideas having a million different stories
if seen from the eyes of the world?

Truth.

SHARPAY EVANS
Shakespeare
Anne
WOODSHOP
CIRCE
MORSE
ARTi
FROZEN THE MOVIE
Ray Bradbury
BOTONY
EMMA
Sherlock Holmes
THE W
GRIMM
Emma
HOUSE OF THE Kurves
Dictionary

The Enchanting things that are Books

Blotched ink turned to typed text,
Through the years everything changed books were true and steady.
Stories bleeding from page to page,
In an enchanting bind of bits and bobs,
Each one telling tales of wonder and excitement,
Encounters and adventures from each era and age,
Each page with its own sparkle and glamour,
Countless epics and wars of rage.

In a sentence the world could come crashing down,
Or the heroes could emerge victorious,
True lovers could find each other amidst darkness,
Or the villains could duel their last.

I could spend years stuck in the pages of books,
Etched into their folds like stamped words,
Living in imagined lands - figments of another's imagination,
Savouring the escape from my own reality,
Surrounded by characters, people and their fervorous recollections,
Teleported to another world.

Such is the fantastical magic of books and tales,
Weaving stories and chronicles into epic tomes,
For children and their kin to enjoy throughout the years,
And have them to hold in times of fear.

14-11-2023

Fear

I no longer live surrounded by fear,
Silent tears streaking down my cheeks,
I no longer bubble with anger and hate,
Procrastination doesn't stain my weeks.

No more do I stare at blank pages,
Wondering how I lost so much time,
No longer do I shudder and sweat,
At the prospect of reading time.

I don't miss a single second,
Of each hour and each day,
I don't struggle to now find peace,
Through the pages containing Faraday.

I say adieu to months spent in repent,
Poring over listlessly, flipping covers,
I say adieu to the longing I felt,
Stuck in my room in the middle of summer.

23.07.24

Stormy

I'm the calm before the darkest storm,
Thoughts and visions suffocating my days,
Thunder coursing through my veins,
As I put up an icy mask, a cool exterior, a stoic face.

I'm tranquility before chaos ensues,
Stuck in oppressive musings,
Trapped in a loop that envelopes me,
Digging its paws into my feelings.

The blush on my cheeks hides the bubbling in my veins,
The impassive gaze compels the listener away,
The smile playing on my lips contradicts the hate in my words,
No one can see the pain that my heart truly incurs.

20.07.2024

Mama

I'll never understand the pain my mother feels,
The tears she hides behind dazzling smiles,
The hidden sorrow she always conceals,
The way her love travels a thousand miles.

I'll never understand her selflessness,
Her ability to give up the very last piece,
The way she holds me ever so dear,
The look in her eyes when she sees me at peace.

I'll never understand her eternal love,
A compassion that knows no bounds,
I'll never understand why the word Ma,
Is the most resonant sound.

21.09.2024

Ma

Ma,

The most resonant word in my vocabulary,

The constant emotional support,

A star in an endless sea of darkness,

Calm waters in a turbulent stream,

Comfort in a storm,

Certainty in chaos,

Truth amidst farce,

Joy in a moment of grief,

The star atop the Christmas tree,

A rose in a bed of thorns,

Treasure in a box of dust,

A diamond in the rough,

Refuge in a perplexing condition,

A shoulder to cry on,

A compass on a lost track and

Love in a world full of hate.

I love you ma, more than yesterday,
less than tomorrow, always and forever.

11.12.2023

Football

How hilarious it is to witness a game of football,
To see grown men squabble over inflated leather,
To see them fall over each other, loose their dignity,
Kissing the grass, falling to their knees,
Such antics to trivially kick an orb,
After all, it's nothing but a game of gall.

11.07.202

Golden

I'll never forget the look on his face,
The dazzling smile, the sparkle in his gaze,
His surprise projected as mock rage,
As I entered his house in a blinding daze.

I'll never forget the tinkle in his laughter,
The way he smiled, always a charmer,
The way he always wanted us close,
And the way he made us love him the most.

07.07.2024

GTO
MO·PA7

Cruising

It's s a funny thing how I attached I am to roads,
The driveways and streets,
The twists and turns.

I like setting off into the sunset,
Leaving behind the rest of the world,
A bonnet in my hair, the wind making it twirl.

Sometimes the drive is serene and silent,
making me want to go back home,
Sometimes it's a symphony of old rhymes and show tunes,
The sun dancing on the car's glossy dome.

I revel in the bliss of sleepy serendipity,
I could stay endlessly, comforted by air-conditioned luxury,
But some days I wish for a glittering red Mustang,
That I could drive in the buttery summer breeze.

I wish to drive and drive to the ends of the world,
Looping through tunnels and lanes,
Scouring the streets for a fuel pit stop,
Racing against the trains.

I dream of the day with my convertible,
Driving along a sunny bay,
Boney M.'s Sunny playing in the background,
While the air smells like a perfumed bouquet.

02.07.2024

Bibliophile

There was once a writer who grew up in the house beside the rails,
Her head was stuck amongst the clouds,
Immersed in some fairytale.

She spent her days cooped up in a room,
She watched the flowers on her window bloom,
She'd read and read from dark to noon,
Stitching the words into her memory's loom.

And so, the stories and tales she read,
Made her want to share her's as well,
And so, one day she sold her ware,
And listened as her patron said,

I believe one day will come to be,
When you will be a great writer indeed,
From your pages eloquence shall bleed,
And from the sown seed you shall reap.

These thoughts and words rang through her head,
As she twisted and turned in her bed,
And to this day she can never forget,
The charming words the man once said.

A bibliophile's heart is forever in books,
No matter the way people look,
It's a way of life, holed up in a nook,
Our forever campion is a dusty book.

And a writer's tales are an expression, an emotion,
Bound to bring about a certain notion,
A story may be of a mountain or an ocean,
But a writer's words are a figment of their devotion.

This is the story of a bibliophile-writer.

16.06.2024

War

War.

Devastation.

Desolation.

Isolation.

Futile by all means yet the source of the world's greatest treasure,

It's History

So vast in its ways, its magnanimity illusionary,

Its secrets and lies alluring even the weakest of intellect.

War.

A notion rife throughout the centuries - brooding, bruising, controlling, contorting, confusing.

What do they tell the soldiers, willing to give their lives for their countries that are nothing but glorified pieces of land?

Land that will no longer sustain the humanity that exploits it endlessly if so, it wishes.

Do they force upon them the truth- the reality?

Do they tell them that their lives would mean nothing to megalomaniacs who'd sell their souls for a taste of power?

Do they tell them that they are nothing but pawns on a checkered board, bartered in the name of "THE GREATER GOOD"?

Nothing but the hope of an illustrious career and a glorious life span to console the Guinea pigs- raised to one day be a 'Warrior'

And what of the common beings?

Homes destroyed, families astray, children abandoned and the dead
decayed.

Centuries old fields are crumbled, and carnage is beheld,

Where once a child's evening was spent in gregarious abandon,

There lie a fractured family's fragments.

The fortunate who return are not as fortunate as believed,

Dust covers their scabbed underlying wounds that don't show but
never heal.

Zest and chants conceal pale faces and white livers,

Forcing the juvenile to hide their shivers,

They kiss goodbye the hopes of a white picket fence,

Bid adieu to a childhood barely spent.

The ones who flee are labeled traitors but were they not robbed of a
right to be free?

They had a choice you say but did they truly?

What is the cost of their freedom?

Shots slice mercilessly through flesh that was once a father, a son, a
hope, a home, a family.

Whatever will free them from dreams that imprison them, haunt them,
torment them endlessly?

Forever seeing the faces, they could've conserved.

Courage, they liquidate but it's never been enough.

Why fight wars that will never wear? Aren't they a bluff?

Pain and grief have bled through the generations,

Ancestral fallacy their true heirloom,

Old prejudice seeking space in the tiniest crevices of their hearts

Forming differences and distances just because of a mark.

Innocents slaughtered in a war between powers,

Their insatiable hunger destroying all that is there to live for,

Don't they know that ultimately nothing is left?

What remains to rule if all is lost?

Unrest, ruin and an endless desire.

To what end?

To what end?

To the army who spends each day as if it's their last,

And yet have hearts and humor we can never surpass.

To the innocents who never knew they'd lose everything they ever had,
who spend sleepless nights and endless days sifting through rubble that
confines their tribe.

To the cruel reality that has created war, and all the futile wreckage it
has caused,

I ask again- what is its cost?

06.01.2024

Tecnología

Entrapped by the innovation we refer to as technology,
We spend our hours and days glued to screens,
Screens that mirror our thoughts and emotions,
Created to cater to our every need.

One text turns to hour long chats,
"Just one reel" leads to hundreds in our feed,
The minutes add up to hours that add up to days and we realize we've reached nowhere.

Time.

Four people in a room, not one striking a conversation,
Each one tip tapping edited colloquies, none interested in a physical tête-à-tête.

Activities once done under the bright yellow sun,
Are now conducted in a room lit azure.
With heaps of blankets both digital and corporeal,
Concealing and trapping all intentions true.

Closed.

Away from a glorious world's treats and treasures,
Stuck in an endless loop each day,
Watching and observing everything yet nothing,
Because what's a page if read through a screen?

Wonders fantastical out there to see,
But we choose to look through another's periphery.

Original thoughts flow no more.
When clouded by others' judgment, we find our foe.

Flowing in a vast sea of half knowledge,
We are but a tiny speck in a glittering, raging ocean,
Dark and odious if we go far enough,
Attracted by the surface that glitters but is not gold.

Deception.

Time and time again we are drawn to the devices,
An addiction I say like no other,
Will we ever be free of it?
I wonder.

Trapped.

10-08-2023

Couleurs

Every colour is beautiful,

Each one has a unique vibrancy,

Like the colour of roses, blush, blood and red,

Like buttercups, canary, buttery and lemony,

Like orange blossoms, burnt, pumpkin and azure,

Like love, pink, cherry and cerise,

Like grass, crisp, apple, jungle,

Like the sky, bright, pale frost, midnight,

Like amethyst, sparkly, Heliotrope, violet,

Like pearls, vanilla, Dutch and eggshell lace,

Like chocolate eyes, caramel, burnt sugar,

Like an obsidian, glittering, onyx, olive, opium.

Each colour an identity,

Each hue an emotion,

Evolving,

Melting,

Bursting.

couleurs.

12.05.2024

Splendour

Luxury, comfort, expense, opulence.

Like the darkest chocolate,

The finest wine,

The oldest whiskey,

The plushest silk,

Like midnight blue- Indigo in sunlight,

Like caramel eyes dripping with desire,

For glitters and trinkets, gems and jewels,

For gossamer draperies, flowers and perfumes,

Such dazzling whims and fancies surround us-

Befriended by diamonds and kisses,

My oh my, whatever will I do, if given a box of such riches?

05.05.2024

Colours of Home

Panchaali- Spirit of the Land

There was once a girl born from fire,
Her persona as fiery as the flame,
Prophesied to change the world with her ways,
Determined to change man's idea of fame.

From a little princess wide eyed and curious,
Tamed, but only in vain,
She questioned each law, each ideal, each custom,
Bemused by the patriarchal ways.

Through endless nights she told her brother tales,
In the morning she'd bat away prying hands,
Until one day a flowered braid displeased the girl,
And she wished for a man to whisk her away to his land.

And so, she met a great sage,
Who promised she'd cause the end of The Age,
He said she'd marry five times over,
And cause millions of widows terrible heartache.

Distraught she wished to dispel this fate,
Desperate to change her future,
The sage knew nothing he did could help,
The woman who'd cause the world to rupture.

And so, he told her to beware of a time,
When she'd be faced with trials,
To hold back her question, her laughter and her curse,
And change the course of destiny.

Leaving the sage we now know as Vyasa,
To write the story of her life,
She thought each day of the five men she ought,
To please one day as a wife.

Her naive dreams compelled her to find, an archer,
who was wise, brave and virtuous,
To find a man who swept her right off her feet,
But she was told she'd never find a Prince,
Who possessed each of these feats.

And so came the Sawyamvar, that changed it all,
Her first test to contain her thoughts,
But she failed miserably when she chose a Pandava,
And insulted a brooding, kshatriya lord.

And so began the series of events,
That led to the war in Kurukshetra,
That changed the face of history itself,
As they witnessed Vyasa's orchestra.

Wed to five indigenous brothers,
Each the epitome of virtues,
She found what one man could not satisfy,
Her desired qualities in each Kuru.

But the blind king could not contain,
His jealous anger at being shunned,
And so, he divided his kingdom in two,
Leaving the Pandavas a wasted van.

But there they built a palace like no other,
Its illusions mystified each onlooker,
It's facades and facets, similar to none,
But no longer open to inviting the ton.

Harmony seemed etched in their lives,
Until a yajna stirred the pot,
The Queen now failed the test yet again,
As she watched the evil spawn fall in a pond.

Now left embarrassed, shamed and hurt,
Anger coursing through her veins,
She vowed to not rest, nor brush her hair,
Until she made the enemy's blood rain.

One day finally came, destined and foretold,

A war that shook the ground itself,

As millions died, thousands were widowed,

And the Queen found sorrow in the mess she created herself.

She later laughed at her naivety,

Her foolishness in disregarding the sage,

Her ire at the way she used love as a balm,

To soothe the ego, she now came to hate.

Once asked are you happy now Panchaali,

She responded with a question of her own,

It was never answered so she questioned always,

"What did it feel like to touch a God?",
the vengeful queen would never know.

Surrounded by folly, patriarchy and schemes,

She was a mind unlike others,

Her curiosity was as amok and as it was keen,

Panchaali, envied by the deities, was the Queen of all Queens.

03.09.2024

Charm In The Chaos

Lights, music, charm and treats,
Stalls filled with goods, bright and sweet,
Ivory bangles of lac, shimmering with gold,
Marvelous wares for one and all.

People of all castes and creeds,
Swarm around, gay and free,
Such simple pleasures they enjoy,
Coloured finery, they employ.

Children abandon all cares and worries,
Liberated by the endless ecstasies.
Merchants call out with discounted guarantees,
Twinkling lights and bombs making up a sight to please.

The festive crowds have let go of burdens many,
Finding solace in Time's brief tarry
Families united yet many stay afar,
Unable to catch a flight or maybe a heart?

Yet a ticking clock bodes ill,
So, we wish time would stay still.

For we wish to paint a picture of the moment,
Capture it in our palm forever,
To cherish, to protect, to remember,
That glorious day in early November.

When the cold misty day was cloaked by the hues,
Of red, yellow, orange and blue.
The colours blurred by fragrant incense,
Food stalls glimmering with decadence and steel,
Attracting those wanting a quick meal.

Such lively spectacles can only be found,
In the festive carnivals in India; all around.

12-30-2023

Bharat

What is India?
Is it culture and spice?
Is it the cobbled streets
Or the corporate mice?

Is it the lush greens or the darkening seas?
Is it narrow alleys or the dancing trees?

Is it home to many or none at all?
Is it someplace magical where rain drops fall?

Is it the children in slums with no means to grub?
Or is it the ones with no one to love?

Is it the land of freedom or none at all?
Is it the democratic place sought by all?

Is it the darkened streets that pose danger to all?
Or the place where lives end once and for all?

Is it the fresh smell of the flowers in bloom?
Or is it the cigarette smoke blown in a plume?

Is it hierarchy, bribery and more?
Or is it the place I call home?

I'll tell you the truth its all of the above,
Even if it may sound rough.

It is the place where diversity is power,
It's my home, Hindustan.

15.08.2022

Love

L.O.V.E

Love is when even a moment away kills you,
When a touch could make you simmer,
A small wave could make your heart flutter,
When a Monday is no longer blue.

Love is hope when the future seems bleak,
A balm amidst a battlefield,
A drop of whiskey in the dark and cold,
A love story that cannot be retold.

Love-in its wake flowers bloom,
The pitter-patter of raindrops, the smell of monsoon,
As delicate and fragile as a daffodil,
So easily crumpled by one's palm at will.

It is a promise of now-not tomorrow, not another day,
It is fleeting as a bird's song, sweet in its own way.
It is a cacophony of colours- blinded yet shaded with a hue,
Love colours our lives, this love so true.
-How do I contain you?

28.04.2024

Brown Eyes

They gaze into my eyes seeing the memories of my past,
Expressing the soft anger they believe the brown orbs hold,
But I wonder why they don't feel the joy they hold inside,
The way the stories form in a chocolate swirl.

How come the mischief doesn't dance for them?
How come the sun doesn't light them up?
How come they don't perceive the molten darkness I see,
Glittering with the laughter of a buttercup.

30.07.2024

elle t'aime

As the sun lit up the hazel in her eyes,

The chocolate swirling with golden lies,

She lifted her fingers to her lips,

As she bid him farewell with a flying kiss.

~I know your love is tortured bliss.

11.07.2024

As he slid his thumb across the gash on her cheek,

He felt an emotion, so complex, so deep,

When a faint blushed crept upon him did he speak,

I'll love you for all of eternity.

11.07.2024

Nature

Simple Pleasures

I think of the simple pleasures in life,
Like going on a walk in the great outdoors,
Chasing a squirrel, climbing a tree,
Painting the sky, hearing tales of yore.

I think of playing a sweet tune on the grand piano,
Of dancing carelessly in the rain,
Of smelling the dew on blades of grass,
Of folding a crisp sheet into a crane.

I think of spending a lazy afternoon,
Drunk over endless cups of tea,
And I think of enjoying a simple ice cream cone,
As I gaze at the trees swaying in the breeze.

I think of tiny bursts of joy,
The adrenaline felt in a pillow fight,
And I wonder where the moments go by,
How we haven't got a slice of time.

I think of the simple pleasure in life,
Like the warmth of a blanket on a chilly day,
And I think of the bright smiles I've saved,
For the rainy days when the sky turns grey.

I wonder when we lost sight of the littlest things,
Succumbing to mechanical routines,
And I wonder how we fail to remember,
That a simple day has become just a dream.

13.08.2023

Heat waves

Skin sticky, hair slick,

Fists clammy, cheeks pink,

Temperatures rising, plants turning sick,

Sweet treats melting into gooey ick.

The sun burning bright and gold,

All one wishes for is something cold,

Now the stories far and old,

Underneath the stars are not told.

Oh! The heat -it burns, it beats,

It takes away all the flair,

Do tell how one can fare,

In this hot and humid air?

16.06.2024

Trees

Green moss and green tress,
Dancing and swaying in the breeze.
Like nothing is wrong, without a flaw,
And all is calm and peaceful for all.
But little do we know,
What happens to the trees we grow.
They don't just wither away from old age,
But are cut with an axe just for a page.
They can't speak but they too feel,
The harsh chops of the axe, and then they kneel.
If they could speak, they would scream,
For mercy and for self-esteem.
But my, oh my they can never run,
For they must face the human gun.

And though we can't say we feel the same,
But maybe we can put out the flame.
The flame that turns trees to ashes,
It feels like the deadliest gashes.
So do you know what the tress must feel,
When man doesn't care to be genteel.
And they suffer and suffer but can't express,
The pain, the hurt and the distress.
So why can't we try our best,
To make an effort and protest.
This situation is getting out of hand,
It must be forbidden; it must be banned.

23.05.2021

Tulip

You are a tulip,

Freshly bloomed,

Lighting up the fields,

With your glorious hue.

Like sunlight blooms a waning sunflower,

Like laughter lights up the murkiest hour,

Like a gossamer blossom,

That brings a blush to one's cheek,

You are a tulip,

Each facet is unique.

24.05.2024

These Hills Have Eyes

The smell of pine overpowered,
The birds chirped; the trees towered.

The temple bells rang,
A sweet song they sang,
The incense seemed to empower,

Raindrops fell, Na-Bi flew,
People prayed for wishes true,
Pitterpatter went dew drops,
Water fell from up top,

I see reds and blues and yellows and greens,
Around curving roads ever so steep,
I see water so blue and so deep,
Like it would carry us away on a silken stream.

I see pin wheels and packed streets,
Books, pictures and fine treats,
Every store tells a story,
Every place its own history.

Oh, if I were to paint a scene
I could never portray what I see

It's a moment I can't capture, a moment I can't share
Meant only for the eyes it ensnares…

09.07.2023

Rainy Days

Sleet and rain drenched my bones as I fled to find shelter,

I ran and ran as fast as I could,
Gleaning the rain wouldn't surrender,

And at last, as I ran out of breath,
I opened the door to the warmth inside,

Heaving a sigh of rain-soaked relief,
As I questioned "Where were you all this time?"

03.09.2024

A Ride In The Rain

As I rode the bus surrounded by showers,

The sills teeming with delicate drops,

The rain pelting against the windows,

The pages of my book rustled,

The raindrops fell on the pleats of my skirt,

The sky darkened to an unruly gloom,

But nothing could dampen my joyful mood,

As I rode the bus through twisting lanes,

Faltering at each bump in the road,

I smiled as the drops touched my cheek,

And washed my worries away.

~ Dear rain, don't go away.

03.09.2024

Contemplation

So fast each one's life passes by,
Each day timed down to the very second,
No longer do we take time to stop,
Never letting our schedule bend.

Why don't we now sit by the lake,
Enjoying the silence and a bit of cake,
Why are moments defined only by words,
And not by the joyful stillness of worlds?

Why is it that we're stuck in a race,
Beating ourselves over nothing,
Continuing to exist in a pace unbeatable,
Rushing, huffing, puffing.

Forever caught in an endless loop,
Responsibility and strain settling on our shoulders,
As if the entire world set us to fail,
And rolled down its terrifying boulders.

Why not take a moment to stay,
And watch the stars in the sky,
Why not jump into the ocean running,
Why not contemplate over chai?

Why don't we now take time to flop,

Into the pools and over the beds,

Why do we contain each wild emotion,

And leave it stuck in our heads.

Why don't we jump into muddy puddles,

Dance carelessly in the rain,

Why do we no longer collect sheets of paper,

And set paper boats to sail.

Why are our mornings a rushed affair,

Hopping from stop to stop,

Why is it that we can no longer take a break,

And watch some bunnies hop?

Why not huddle beneath the covers,

And read a cozy book,

Why not spend late nights gazing,

At the twinkling stars we overlook.

Why not sit by the riverside,

A blanket to cover us from the breeze,

The sun shining, the water running,

And berries hanging from the tops of trees.

Let us take some time to love ourselves,

And love each thing around.

Let's take some time to sit about.

And step away from the crowd.

21.06.2024

A Sprightly Dance in The Rain

I love the feeling of dancing in the rain,

The raindrops disguising my tears,

The feeling of carefree abandon,

Pitter-patter drenching our frames.

I love the feeling of the cool water,

Swirling and dancing on my face,

I love the way I feel alive,

Amongst the trees ablaze.

I revel in these monsoon showers,

Grateful for a moment alone,

Sopping and squelching in the thunderous squall,

Drenching the voices of the unknown.

I dote on the bright orange hues,

The flurry of colours in the flora,

I taste the wondrous dew drops they pour,

Enveloped by their trembling aura.

12.07.2024

Death

Daze

As she told me she'd passed away,
I felt so numb- as if in a daze,
My movements forced, mechanical,
Muscle memory leading the way.

Tears didn't escape, however,
As my brain couldn't relate,
"What has happened?" I asked- lost,
Of this day I was afraid.

18.07.2024

Death

Someone passes away who's near and dear,
Tear filled eyes and sobbing we hear.

A white sheet ablaze with flame,
Yellow and red burning away the blame.

As the ashes turn to dust,
Blown away in the wind, light as dust.

Leaving behind worldly sorrows,
Looking forward to the morrow.

And after the day that we part,
Time, Healing along the scarred, broken heart.

I keep you alive in my memories,
The good, bad and ugly in my treasury.

Knowing I will soon see you again,
To hold tight and never let go again.

04.08.2022

Heartbreak

Months have gone by, yet the pain perseveres,
Minutes turn to hours but my heart doesn't seem to heal.

Sleepless nights turn to endless days,
I wish for just another minute with him.

A second chance.
Another glance.
An embrace.
A laugh.

I desire.

I try to cover up, look pretty, seem fine,
But my grief envelopes me, it consumes me whole, I die.

I try.

All it takes is a memory, a word,
When I think I've got it together my heart bursts,
I feel a metal knife, icy, lethal, hack at me,
I feel it puncture my organs making them endlessly bleed,

I feel lost, alone, afraid.
Alone in an endless void of darkness.

I give into oblivion, and I wonder,
I wonder, I wonder, I wonder
When will I feel whole again?

I ask myself, I ask Yahweh, I ask pale death,

Will it ever end?
Will the chaos reign?
With this gaping hole in my breast ever heal?
Will I ever be free of this feeling that binds me,
Restricts me, chokes me and tortures me,

When will I be free?
I cry.

Hopeless thoughts overpower,
Every minute, every second, every hour.

They suck me into their vicious trap yet,
I resist their temptation, I control, I smile.

But is it all a ruse, a game, a trick? I question.

I'm chaos, I'm ruin, I'm undone.
I'm trapped in an endless raging battle,
I parry, I block, I defend, I strike, I loose.
Bit by bit I break.
If only I stopped feeling.

I'm numb.
I feel desperate, desolate, alone in a vast sea of sorrow,
But I embrace the confusion,
I revel in the fire that burns me, soothes me, creates me.

I ask. I cry. I burn. I feel.

It makes me mortal.
It makes me vulnerable.
Death.

03.08.2023

Quietus

How do I deal with this solidarity?
Knowing that at the end of it all you have everything, yet nothing.

How do I escape the burning, aching grief that envelopes me each day,
each hour, each second,
Like hell fire from the pits, charring, demolishing, fiery, blazing.

Oblivion is my being, my state of living- if living is what you call it,
Passing days become blurred memories,
A constant fog- blinding, caging, threatening, uncertain,

Lost.

How sick and yet how true is this game of life,
Harsh and yet the only certainty there is.

Truth.

Life and its fickleness allude me.
It's like each one is dying since the morning we see,
Each one of us living in the absence of something else,
Finding echoes of what used to be,

A slip and slide into the darkness,

I now wonder if really, happiness can be found by simply turning on the light?

I ask these questions as I implore the world to answer,

I knock on the doors of heaven and hell, for a brief word, a simple meaning,

A remedy for this grief.

I'm tired of carrying its burden and I'd sell my soul to be relieved.

They try to protect me but how long will the shield last?

How long until the gashes, the scars, the knives, the fire finally crack it open, and I'll be exposed to the thunderous battle that is coping with death.

Thoughts are looping, turning, collisions - striked through over and over again until the page rips - all in vain for that unfathomable key.

I know there are people listening, but does anyone have an answer?

Afraid.

Alone.

Quietus.

Escape.

Torture.

Grief.

01.05.2024

Departure

How cruel is the departure of the dead,
Their place cleared out for another set,
Their ashes- barely cleared, are whisked away,
To make space for the next one to go away,

Phantom tears are caressed away,
Lost in memory, amidst disarray,
Eyes bright and wishes fly away,
In hope that tomorrow will be a better day,

In hope that tomorrow will be a better day,
Where we're allowed to mourn- allowed to stay,
To kiss the brow of the forever slumbered,
To know they'll never come back,
Yet hold onto hope anyway.

17.04.2024

Grief

Where Are You Now?

I held his cold body,
Kissed his icy face,
So frail and delicate his form,
Once the strongest in the space.

He looked ever so small,
So, at peace,
At last, at rest,
His wondrous look lost.

Glassy eyes unseeing,
Unsettling was his gaze,
My sister's childish innocence,
Forbid her from an embrace.

His startlingly grey eyes,

That once pierced my soul,

Now no longer glowed with life,

The fire of rage and the kindle of warmth,

Extinguished, butchered as if by a knife.

His large hands that once blessed my head,

Now lay still by his side,

His demeanour, once commanding,

Now diminished was the swagger, hidden was the pride.

His comforting words now silenced,

His sparkling eyes no longer danced,

His laughter now echoed only in memories,

His wisdom forever in our hearts.

10.03.2024

Strange Affairs

It's strange how this process of grief works,

One moment it engulfs you, consumes you torments you,

In another, it passes, soothing, gentle.

I dare say I feel happy, for a brief moment,

But alas, fear grips at me, hurting me.

Afraid.

The one who passed becomes a faint memory,

An illusion I once believed to be true.

Now his name doesn't make me cry,

His memory feels so distant- awry

I'm scared I'll lose the feeling of his love,

His affection, comfort, words and such,

Fear I'll forget the sound of his voice,

Ringing through my ears as I entered his house of wonder,

In trepidation I stay of forgetting his stories,

Often told swinging amongst the trees,

Doubting my evocation, is part of the daily
routine- how misgiving is an echo.

Fear.

Dear dread I command you, beseech you, implore you
To set us free of your trap,
Let us go in peace and tranquility,
Content in the memories from the past.

Stop the madness, the insanity, the profanity,
Give me freedom.

I demand it.

But do I deserve it?
Strange affairs.

12-04-23

Solidarity

Solitude

Friendship.

What is it really?

Is it a warm embrace on a chilly day?

A phone call, a click away?

A shoulder to cry on-

A person to rely on-

A text at 12 or a coffee at Ben's?

What really is a friend?

I think about mine and I feel lost,

They're a click away yet it feels like there are miles between us.

All I feel good for is a text because where are they when I'm drowning,

When I need a hand-a rant-a shoulder?

I wouldn't know if you asked- who's your friend?

I ask myself the same.

Me, myself & I

That's MY reality.

But maybe I'm okay with it.

I find myself lonesome, desolate, lost, afraid, a dim light in a vast
expanse of darkness.

I see no light tethered to me to bring me back from the shallows.

Is it me?

What do I lack?

I see gaggles of friends,

Keeping up with the trends,

Is that the definition of a friend?

I see people comforting the inconsolable,

Listening to the cries, the sorrow, the grief,

And I think that's a bosom friend indeed.

I'm lost to the concept that is camaraderie.

Tell me, please tell me what it really is.

Alone.

I keep asking but no answer comes my way.

Each person with their own fickle customs,

Differences and assumptions.

So, I question myself,

Do I really have a friend?

Maybe I'm meant to be my own companion.

23-08-2023

Oh! If I Were A Bird

If I were a bird, given the wings to fly,

The freedom to soar, to explore heavens anigh,

I would spread my wings and take to the skies,

Feel the cool air and view the sights.

To be unbound by the restraints of humanity,

The restrictive social customs, discrimination-I would be free, I would
be content,

If I were a bird.

They have no religion, no caste nor creed,

All they have is family, whom they work hard to feed.

They have no god, no pariah, no saviour,

They fend for themselves, they parry, they block, they act as defenders.

They have no war, no hate, no feuds,

Why not partake in their world?

Oh! If I were a bird.

Whilst we were locked by spread of contagion, they soared freely the
sky so blue,

With no fear of disease, with houses in trees,

What a beautiful human free world they see,

When up in the sky, feeling the breeze.

Oh! If I were a bird.

How does it feel to live in trees?

To bite into fruits straight from the branch?

To be forever surrounded by the fauna and the bees?

To wake up to the dropping dew in the morn,

With no unruly neighbours or cars with horns.

Oh, how blissful it would be,

To live amongst the fluttering, dancing trees.

All such pleasures would be mine,

If only I was a bird.

13-05-2023

Deserving?

I don't expect to be treated better,
Or even be treated fairly.

I don't think I deserve the way I'm coddled,
Or even the way they support me.

I don't feel like I deserve their love,
Their words of appreciation, affections and such,

I feel like I should resist their kisses and hugs,
Their timeless laughter and gales of love.

8.8.2024

Rejection

Rejection bitter, hot strikes along my face,

Leaving a gaping, bleeding gash,

As I spend a moment to contemplate,

When I'll win this conniving race.

06.08.2024

I Don't Care

I don't care if I'm not a part of the crowd,
Or if I don't go dancing around town.
I don't care if I sit alone at lunch,
Or if I don't interact with the popular bunch.

I don't mind if I'm unable to strike a conversation,
Or if I can't seem to crack a joke,
I don't mind if my hellos are ignored,
Or if my passions make you snore.

I don't care if the crowd stays quiet,
Or if the applause doesn't seem so wild,
I don't care if someone sees me cry,
Or if they're oblivious, their comfort awry.

I don't care if I'm scrutinized or feared,
Or if the kids find me icy and weird.
I don't care if I win or lose,
Or if I'm not dancing to Footloose.

I don't have feelings, I'm doomed, I'm despair,
I'm not constantly badgered by people who compare.
And what I don't care about most is that I don't care at all,
I don't care a little bit,
Not even at all.

02.08.2024

Validity

Sunny days have lost their luster,
Gloomy rooms, thick heavy books and classes form my days,
It's endless hours of meetings, tests, analyses and activities,
All to form the perfect foundation for the rest of my life.

Thinking years ahead has become a way of life,
Each mistake is criticized, scrutinized, trife,
The tension builds like a boiling cauldron,
On the brink of overflowing, causing such strife.

The bus rides once jolly and breezy are no more enticing,
A reprieve from the hustle and bustle, a moment to breathe,
Half an hour to catch up on lost sleep,
Awake physically but we're really asleep.

Just another year they say but the competition never ends,
Each one ditching the other to get ahead, to take the test, be the best.

In the merciless cycle of education and competition

We're starved of the childhood pleasures we once enjoyed,

Drowning under the pressure of applications and choices,

Racing for that extra point five,

We give up on humility, compassion and integrity.

Doing anything, we can, to achieve our means,

Disregarding human tendencies and emotions like robots on a quest,

Our thirst for power is never quenched.

Community connect, competitions and friends are nothing
more than contracts,

Another achievement for a sheet of paper we try so hard to perfect.

The constant burden of acceptance, inclusivity and perfection weighs
down on me like a million bricks,

I'm stuck in the endless cycle of thousands of Homosapiens running
towards a single target,

Trampling over hearts and people in their way in a ruthless
battle to the top

And for what I ask?

Validation.

Locked

Locked boxes and marked floors,
Bolted locks and sealed doors,
Secrets zipped and pursed lips,
Abandoned criers and slits in bricks.

Such is our natural reflex,
Bound to be fickle and untrue,
Taught to lock people out, yet pick our locks ourselves,
Conditioned to drown out the voices knocking in our head.

We've learnt to not let them in,
Put up a solid wall of brick,
Trapping ourselves behind the facade,
Locking out those reaching into our hearts.

No longer do we spew the truth,
So used to lying through our teeth,
Terrified of the hurt a person could inflict,
If led through our wall of deceit.

Locked.

02.05.2024

Ocean

The ocean that once invited me with open arms now scares me.
Its waves dark and ominous, threaten my very being.
Its magnanimity alludes me, its endlessness terrifies,
Once so calm and still it seemed,
Now a turbulence it's deemed.

Vast is its swathe, its depth illusionary,
Are my fears true or just imaginary?

Do I fear oblivion and the truth of the unknown?
Yes, I do, and that the ocean knows.
Its nature scares me yet makes me aware,
One wrong step and its tide ensnares.

So am I wrong in being afraid of the dark,
Afraid of the murky depths but not of the sky of stars?
Afraid of the secrets hidden in the gloom,
Afraid of the uncertainty to bloom.
Hidden are the secrets of the ocean and its ways,
Many a people tried but all lost their way.

Change.
Illusion.
Fear.

17.02.2024

Subtlety

How slow paced was life back in the days,
The leisure in lazy opulence,
And although I can't say I witnessed the same,
My imagination makes up for the same.

The music seemed softer,
The harmonies deeply resonant,
The subtle romance that hid behind the covers,
Can't be seen in the gardens again.

Shy voices no longer beckon,
One to their allure and charm,
What once was a world with delicate pleasure,
No longer cherishes loving arms.

3.9.24

The Story

The Bhutta

My grandfather had various jobs throughout his life. He was a milkman by day and a storyteller by night. During the summers, he would sell corn on the cob, roasted over coal on a beat-up wooden rickshaw, and during the long, hard winters, he would chop wood until his hands turned blue from the cold. But through all the hardships he faced in his day-to-day life, trying his best to provide for his family, he would always come back with a sweet treat—a small cob of leftover corn—and a bedtime story to enchant me. His favorite tale, however, was the one about how he found me.

Before you assume I'm adopted, I am not. My father, who was a drunk, good-for-nothing layabout, once quarreled with my grandfather over money. He had run out of funds to quench his thirst for alcohol and had no alternative but to ask my grandfather for some. When my grandfather refused, he grabbed hold of my flailing, bony arms and carried me out of our mud home as I wailed sharply in the chilly night. Months passed as my father exploited me for money. He would make me beg on the streets for hours in the scorching heat until I would pass out from exhaustion, my blistered feet unable to carry me further. He left no money to spare for food, and we often went to sleep without even a bite to eat.

It was a harsh winter that year. The little rations I had scrounged up were gone, and there was little to shield me from the cold besides a thin, torn shawl. I was certain I would die. But somehow, I survived the dreary winter months. My father, however, did not. His addiction had finally overtaken his malnourished body, leading to his somewhat expected death. I was truly alone then. No neighboring family would take me in—too burdened by their own children to spare a morsel for me—so I begged some more, trying not to starve.

One day, a fair, white lady found her way through the slum and brought me to a children's shelter. At the Saint Paul Shelter for the Homeless, I was provided with hot meals three times a day, a room to share with several other raggedy children, and a proper education, enabling me to read and write. As the years passed, I grew taller, my hollow cheekbones filled in, and the color returned to my face. But I never forgot my grandfather. His bedtime stories ran through my mind each night as I lay on a mattress on the floor, stray legs surrounding me as I drifted off to sleep. His tales of mighty elephants, slippery snakes, sly foxes, and weightless birds were tiny pieces of his memory that I kept locked inside my heart, unwilling to share them with anyone just yet. They were special—mine to keep forever.

It had been five years since the night my father had taken me away. It was my 12th birthday. That day, several elderly people were brought into the shelter. I searched each one's face, hoping to see my grandfather, but in vain. Dada says he still remembers the look on my face when I saw him walk through the doors of the shelter. He had searched for me all those years, carrying a picture of me in his pocket, showing it to every customer who bought corn from him. By some odd miracle, the same white lady who had rescued me had stopped by his rickshaw to indulge in some piping hot corn and immediately recognized my cheeky face from the stained, yellowed photograph. She had brought my grandfather to the shelter and watched, teary-eyed, as he engulfed me in a rib-cracking hug.

Dada, overjoyed to have found his long-lost grandson, was so overcome with joy that he treated all the kids in the shelter to pieces of patisa. That evening, as my birthday came to an end, we made our way back to the ramshackle mud house we called home and celebrated with a whole bag of sweet treats. My grandfather's old, spotted face, which had aged terribly over the past few years apart, now radiated with the youth of a young man, as he finally told me all the stories, he had left untold.

17.09.2024

www.ingramcontent.com/pod-product-compliance
Lightning Source LLC
Chambersburg PA
CBHW040909110726

48005CB00006B/852